TRAPPED
In The
CONGO DRAMA

TRAPPED
In The
CONGO DRAMA

Raymond M. NGOMA

authorHOUSE®

AuthorHouse™
1663 Liberty Drive
Bloomington, IN 47403
www.authorhouse.com
Phone: 1-800-839-8640

Scripture quotation are taken from the King James Version (KJV) of the Bible-Public Domain

Published by AuthorHouse   12/27/2012

ISBN: 978-1-4817-0346-8 (sc)
ISBN: 978-1-4817-0345-1 (hc)
ISBN: 978-1-4817-0344-4 (e)

Library of Congress Control Number: 2012924289

All the Glory to my GOD,
the LORD JESUS CHRIST
(John 14:1-14).

To all Congo people, victims of international conspiracy
in their country. To all of them who have had their lives
destroyed by the global Mafia.

Contents

Chapter 1

Gilbert Mavinga was a young man originally from the southern part of the Congo Republic. He was a very beautiful and awesome young man who was almost nineteen years of age. He was very intelligent and just graduated from Kouilou High School (Kouilou was the southwestern province of the Congo Republic). He had successfully received his high school diploma, also called *Baccalauréat* in the French education system. He majored in math, management, and accounting.

After his honorable graduation from high school, he was accepted by the Congo Education Ministry to continue studies at University of Brazzaville, in the capital city of the Congo Republic.

At University of Brazzaville, Gilbert was assigned to study business management in the department of economic sciences. But Gilbert still had two months left before he left Pointe-Noire to go to Brazzaville in September.

Pointe-Noire, also called *Ponton-la-Belle*, was the second largest city of the Congo Republic. It was on the edge of the Atlantic Ocean and was the biggest port in open sea. Because of that, it was considered an economic city of the Congo Republic.

Pointe-Noire was also the administrative city of the province of Kouilou. It was where all regional institutions were located, including Gilbert's high school.

Gilbert lived in Pointe-Noire with his parents. Damien and Susan Mavinga were retired. They had five children together, and Gilbert was their fourth child. Their first child's name was Henry; he was a political activist living in Brazzaville, where he worked as a propaganda agent for the party in power. He was twenty-nine.

Henry was considered the financial support of the family in Pointe-Noire, because his parents did not work anymore and he had brothers and sisters to help with school and daily life.

Henry made good money. He was in charge of the communication department for his party, which rules the country. Henry's party was also in charge of the finances of the country. This was the way things worked here. So, Henry didn't have to worry about his salary and bonuses. In Brazzaville he had a nice car in his possession. His party gave him the car. Also, he lived in a big government house, which was managed by the governing party too. This was the reality in this part of the world.

Henry was very happy to prepare a place for his young brother, who just had successfully graduated from high school and was coming soon to live with him and to continue studies at University of Brazzaville.

The joy was totally in the family. Gilbert was the second child to go to university after Henry. The other children in the family were girls, and here girls did not have a great chance to finish high school. Mostly, they ended up getting quickly married to the first gentleman who was able to seduce them first and then their parents. Here, it was always good marry off the daughters instead of letting them prostitute themselves on the street. There was no real way for young ladies to succeed and become somebody for their families or for their country.

Girls were here to seduce, get married, make children, and take care of their families. And men were the ones who got out there, found jobs, got paid, and brought money to the family. If men could bring in more money, then they could traditionally marry many women and live together in the same house. Or they could keep one legally married woman home and then get many other side women they called *bureau*, living in separate houses around the city.

In the countryside, the man who had more plantations, cows, pigs, goats, sheep, and chickens was considered rich. He could get all the women he wanted and keep them all in his house as his wives. It was a tradition in most tribes of the Congo Republic. But today, with the presence of new technologies that bring people closer around the world, many Congo people can check out what's happening in the developed world.

And because of that, things are changing slowly but surely. And many families are now pushing their baby girls to go to school and get a good basic education. And with the help of nongovernment organizations, many young girls are getting degrees and even graduating from university. After university, some of them are getting good jobs, but still the situation must continue to improve, because here, educated or not, women are still considered inferior by proud men.

Chapter 2

As a young man who had just graduated from high school and was about to go to university in Brazzaville, Gilbert was having a very good vacation in Pointe-Noire.

Everybody around him was very proud of him and admired him for his intelligence. The families with young girls were almost pushing them to get in contact with Gilbert. They expected them to become engaged to him. This was because Gilbert had a bright future in front of him. Even families who never talked to Gilbert's family before were doing it now.

But Gilbert was not interested. His mind was set on Brazzaville. He wanted to get there quickly so he could start university.

In the meantime, when Gilbert was having a good time with his friends in the city, something was happening in his parents' house, where he lived. The neighbors had pushed their seventeen-years-old daughter, Monique, to go see Gilbert's mother, Susan, and help her with light housework like washing dishes and cleaning the living room. In the Congolese mentality, it was always good to get in the heart of one's future fiancé's parents before getting in their son's heart.

By sending their daughter to help Gilbert's mother with her housework, Monique's parents were sure their daughter would captivate the hearts of Gilbert's parents, who would convince their son to marry Monique.

Monique stayed with Gilbert's mother for almost half a day. And when Gilbert came back home, he was surprised to see Monique in the house, socializing with his mother.

Monique and Gilbert knew each other very well because they lived next door to each other. But Gilbert never thought of having Monique as his girlfriend. He was always busy attending high school and preparing for his future.

Monique was a very polite and pretty girl. She looked like a real black pearl with small round eyes, a small noise, thick lips, and a very beautiful smile. She had the body of a model, with a well-formed backside and breasts big like oranges. She had dropped out of school in ninth grade. And that was a problem for Gilbert. He always wanted to meet a girl who was at the same education level as him. So it was clear this connection would never work.

But that day, after Monique left and returned to her house, Gilbert's mother started convincing his son to like Monique. She said to Gilbert, "How do you like her? Isn't she beautiful? She is a very nice and polite girl. She knows how to take care of her house. She cleans well and even cooks well. This girl could be a very good fiancée. What do you think?"

Gilbert answered, "Oh yes, Mother, she looks nice." This answer was just to calm his mother down. Anyway, this seemed like a present for Gilbert. He felt happy and wanted to enjoy Monique's presence before he went to Brazzaville.

So, he decided to go out with Monique over the next few days. Gilbert liked her because she talked nicely and had a lot of respect for people and, more importantly, for him.

Imagine the joy that Gilbert's mother and Monique's parents had when they saw them going out together for the first time. Gilbert and Monique saw each other almost every day. Together they went almost everywhere in the city: the beach, the movie theater, a local concert, downtown Pointe-Noire for shopping, and a local football game.

Many girls in the city started to get uncomfortable when they saw Gilbert and Monique walking together. They clearly wished to be in Monique's place. Some of them even said, "What does he sees in this girl? Doesn't he find us more attractive than her? With these bodies! He's really missing a lot."

But Gilbert didn't listen to them. He just cared about his very sweet Monique. For Gilbert's and Monique's families there was no doubt that Monique had become Gilbert's official fiancée.

Chapter 3

It was the end of vacation for Gilbert. He had to prepare his luggage for the trip to Brazzaville. For this purpose, Gilbert went shopping in the city with his parents. Together they had to find a good suitcase and a big, nice-looking travel bag that would fit all Gilbert's new clothes, shoes, books, and other necessities.

At the marketplace called Grand Marché, it was easy to find anything, and prices were low in comparison to the high prices exclusive shops in downtown Pointe-Noire charged for similar things.

Of course, when it came to clothes and shoes, Gilbert never bought them in the popular marketplace. It would be a shame if Monique or others saw him shopping in such a place. He had to look good to go to Brazzaville, which people called nicely *Brazza-la-Verte,* or "Brazzaville the Green City," because there were a lot of trees along the streets and the taxis were all painted green. Also, Brazzaville had many institutions, including the only university in the country and other attractions. Brazzaville was located next to Kinshasa, which was the capital of the Democratic Republic of Congo. With just a document called *Laissez-passer*, an official permit that could be obtained quickly at a local immigration office, one could take the ferryboat across the majestic Congo River in just fifteen minutes and land in Kinshasa, called affectionately *Kin-la-Belle*, meaning "Kinshasa the Beautiful City." For people from Brazzaville, going to Kinshasa was like going to Las Vegas.

For them, shopping in Kinshasa was great because their CFA franc was stronger than the franc of the Democratic Republic of Congo. That's why many people crossed the Congo River daily, especially on weekends, to go to Kinshasa for shopping or a good time.

And people from Kinshasa loved to go to Brazzaville with small merchandise that they sold quickly at the ferryboat port of Brazzaville or even inside the city. The merchandise from Kinshasa was good and was sold cheap to Brazzaville people. This way Kinshasa people made good money in CFA francs.

This kind of activity became crucial for many families. And people from Brazzaville and Kinshasa could easily communicate because they both spoke French and Lingala. (Lingala is a national language spoken in the Congo.)

It was in Gilbert's interest to look good for himself and his parents, who continued to be proud of him. And he did not want to look like a country boy. It was a matter of showing that Gilbert not only was intelligent but also looked like a city boy.

Besides French, which was the official language of the Congo people (especially intellects and students), the people on the streets of Brazzaville spoke mostly Lingala instead of Kikongo. Gilbert didn't know Lingala, only French, Kikongo, and Vili, which was the dialect of the Vili people originally from Diosso, Pointe-Noire. He certainly would speak French, the official language of the country, to communicate, but living in Brazzaville would help him learn Lingala fast. That's what Gilbert thought.

The day after Gilbert had done the shopping, he started packing all his things. He was alone in his room. First, he put in his suitcase all his new pants, new shirts, and some old clothes that still looked good. He had a lot of things left, but the suitcase was already full. In the travel bag he put all his nice shoes, pajamas, toiletries, and other accessories. He also had a large leather handbag in which he packed all his schoolbooks and notes that helped him graduate from high school. Now, he was almost ready to go.

The trip was already set; he had a first-class train ticket for tomorrow at six o'clock in the afternoon. The express train would go about three hundred kilometers between Pointe-Noire and Brazzaville in about twelve hours, which was amazing, because the railroad was only one way and crossed the tough Mayombe (a chain of mountains in the middle of the Congo jungle), and the tracks were not electric. The express train had priority of the principal railroad in the country and only stopped at the major stations.

In the meantime, Gilbert's mother had something to do in the kitchen. She was frying a red snapper and some special chicken parts. She would place this meal in plastic containers so that Gilbert would have something special to eat on the road. Also, she would put aside some strong fried Congo chili pepper.

It was very expensive to buy food in the train restaurant. So people cooked food at home and took it on the road.

People could buy bread, juice, and bottles of water at the Central Train Station. People could buy their *kwanga* (or cassava bread) too, but the tastiest *kwanga* was the one people could buy from local village farmers. The village farmers used to sell their agricultural products at train stations like *Bilinga, Bilala,* and *Mboulou.* The agricultural products that small farmers in the village sold the most were: *kwanga, pondu* (or cassava leaves), cassava tubers, locally grown potatoes, corn cobs, peanuts, palm nuts, sugarcane, and different kinds of vegetables and fruits, like eggplant, onion, garlic, sorrel, mango, banana, pineapple, avocado, *safu* plums, etc.

They also sold dried smoked fish, smoked wild animal meat (like antelope, gazelle, wild boar, buffalo, and monkey), dried or live insects, and caterpillars, crickets, termites, etc. Additionally, they sold fresh wild animal meat, like crocodile meat, boa meat, tortoise meat, wild chicken meat, wild rat meat, etc.

Finally, today Gilbert would be leaving Pointe-Noire.

In the afternoon, everybody was ready to go to downtown Pointe-Noire to the Central Train Station. They had an arrangement with a muni-van driver who would take them all to the train station at four thirty in the afternoon. Monique was among the people who would accompany Gilbert to the train station. Gilbert's parents and sister were there too.

At Pointe-Noire Central Train Station everybody was sad because Gilbert was leaving. But visibly, Gilbert's mother and Monique were more anxious to see Gilbert leaving. Gilbert's dad gave him one last piece of advice on how he should live in Brazzaville.

"Please focus on your studies, and follow what your big brother will tell you. Always follow his advice," said Gilbert's father.

Then Gilbert took his pocket money and asked his sister to buy him bread, a large soda, and one bottle of water. Gilbert's mother was visibly sad to let another kid go far away from them, but there was nothing she could do. When her oldest son, Henry, left them to live in Brazzaville, it was more difficult for her to accept. But thanks to Henry, the family could feel better, especially with the financial support he gave them every month. Also, every six months Henry used to come to Pointe-Noire to visit his parents so they could not really miss him. So there was no fatalism here. Things would be okay for everybody.

All the travelers, including Gilbert, waited for the train to enter the station. Then at five thirty, when the train stopped in the middle of the station, Gilbert and his father took the luggage and carried it to the first-class car. After all Gilbert's things were placed inside his compartment, his father got off the train. That's when Gilbert got time to talk to his Monique, who was already crying, seeing her love about to leave her. Gilbert tried to calm her down, but there was nothing he could do. Gilbert's sister and mother also tried to calm her down, but she continued to wipe tears from her eyes.

Then they heard the first sound of the whistle, instructing passengers to get into their car and sit down, as the train would move soon.

Gilbert kissed his mother and sister, hugged his father, and gave Monique a long good-bye kiss. Then he jumped into his first-class car.

At the third whistle, the train started moving. Everybody waved their hands to Gilbert, who was standing by the window of his compartment. The train left exactly at six o'clock in the evening and would get to Brazzaville at about six o'clock in the morning.

The night came fast. At about seven thirty, the train got to Bilala. At this station many village people made their living by selling their small farm products to travelers.

When Gilbert heard a village lady screaming, *Kwanga, kwanga, kwanga*, he decided to stand up and ask the lady to come to his window. The lady had on her head a big bowl of cassava breads. Gilbert asked the lady to show him a sample of the merchandise before he bought seven *kwangas*.

"These are the best ones," he said. He planned to eat one or two with his fried fish and chicken and leave some as a present for his brother in Brazzaville.

Always during the nighttime, he was able to buy from other train stations some nicely dried and well-smoked catfish, big mangoes, bananas, oranges, a sweet pineapple, eggplants, and coconuts.

After eating his food and contemplating the country landscape, Gilbert fell sleep. He was so comfortable sleeping during the rest of the trip that he couldn't feel the motion of the train.

He woke up at about five o'clock in the morning, when the train was getting close to Brazzaville. It was still dark outside, but he could continue to admire the beauty of the Congo nature.

"We still have about one hour left to get to the destination," he said to himself.

He had never been in Brazzaville, and his heart was now beating fast with emotion. He knew that his brother was waiting for him at the Brazzaville train station. So he was not really worried about that. It was the new environment of the capital city, which made him feel shy and a little scared.

Then the train entered the Central Train Station in Brazzaville. It was exactly ten minutes past six in the morning.

He said suddenly, "Here we go! This is Brazzaville, my new city!"

Gilbert's brother Henry had been there since five thirty in the morning, waiting for his young, brilliant brother to arrive.

Before the train stopped, Henry saw his brother standing by the window, trying to locate him. Henry screamed, "Gil, Gil!" and waved to him.

Gilbert saw him and was assured. He was so happy to see his brother running after the train.

When the train stopped completely, Gilbert started unloading his things from the train and handing them to Henry through the window. It was easy to pass things through the window because the car's main exit door was packed with people. All of them wanted to exit the train at the same time.

After a few minutes, Gilbert came out of the train. The two brothers hugged each other tightly with joy.

Henry said, "Welcome to *Brazza-la-Verte*, little brother!"

Then Henry and Gilbert took his things to Henry's car, quickly left the Central Train Station, and headed to Henry's house. On their way home, Henry asked Gilbert about their family in Pointe-Noire. Gilbert told him everything he wanted to know about them.

Chapter 4

In early September, Brazzaville felt a little cold. It was the dry season. The temperature at this time of the year was between eighteen and twenty-three degrees centigrade in the morning, and between twenty-eight and thirty-two degrees during the daytime. This was really quite mild, as Congo was located right on the equator and had a tropical climate, especially during the intense rainy season.

In the popular zones of Brazzaville, where most people lived and did businesses *à la Congolaise* ("in Congolese way"), things were different from downtown Brazzaville, where modern buildings lined the paved sidewalks. These popular zones include Poto-Poto, Moungali, Ouenze, Plateau, Bas-Congo, Mfilou, Moukondo, Makelekele, etc.

In these areas, the roads to principal streets and avenues were well done. But inside any of these popular communes was disappointing, as the ground was filled with mud during the rainy season and with dust during the dry season. The gutters were open and were not regularly cleaned out. That was why they were always full of sand, stones, debris, and stagnant dark water that smelled bad.

Mosquitoes lingered around this standing water and brought malaria fever to people. It was the country's number-one killer of children. The situation was the same in other big cities, like Pointe-Noire, Loubomo, etc. The future of this country could be at risk of dangerous diseases due to failure of public health services!

People here did not really care about public sanitation in the city. But almost everywhere in the city, loud music played in open bars, where people were sitting and drinking *Primus* and *Ngok,* the two most popular beers of the country. Nothing could affect their love for Brazzaville—not even the mountain of detritus or the standing dirty water in gutters that was always visible.

This environment was part of their life. They worked, drank, ate, and danced here, but they also mourned and cried when there was a death in the family. And life went on. Living in this kind of environment made the charm of life, and this life was all they had.

And now Gilbert was a part of this city's life. His brother's house was located in Plateau. In this area were beautiful houses and wealthy people. This area was close to Gilbert's department of economic sciences. Every day, he would probably walk or take the bus to get there or to get back home. His brother Henry had a busy schedule and would never give him a ride to school.

Classes at University of Brazzaville were free, and each student had monthly financial support of 25,000 CFA francs. This was the amount of money students were receiving in that time, but today nobody knows if they are still getting anything. In his brother's house, Gilbert was given a nice room equipped with a queen-size bed, a desk with a nice rotating chair, a large wardrobe, a clock, and a lamp placed on a small table. In his room Gilbert had placed on the desk all his books and the binders in which he kept important notes. Back then, people didn't have personal computers; otherwise, Gilbert would have had one on his desk.

People didn't have cellular phones either, but they had traditional fixed phones in their living rooms. These phones did not really work properly, especially for outgoing calls. Anytime one had to make a long-distance call to another city like Pointe-Noire, he had to request connection from the office in charge of telecommunications.

Gilbert's brother had one of these. He had put it there just to display it like something in a museum. He didn't use it often, except when he needed to call his parents in Pointe-Noire.

Also Gilbert had placed his shirts and pants neatly in the wardrobe, along with some other things. But the empty travel bag and suitcase were placed on top of the wardrobe. They probably would stay there until the next trip, when he would go back to Pointe-Noire for his first vacation.

Would he really have a chance to go back to Pointe-Noire to spend his first vacation near his family and his girlfriend, Monique? The future would tell.

Today was Gilbert's first day at University of Brazzaville. He could read his name on the department's main information board. He felt so proud and honored to see his family name placed there. It read, "MAVINGA Gilbert, Business Management, First Grade, Group A."

He wrote down his weekly schedule and went quickly to the auditorium for his first business administration class.

In the auditorium, Gilbert was surprised to see so many students from different sections taking the same class as him. The room was very large and could contain more than a thousand people. It was equipped with a microphone, speakers, projectors, a projection screen, a large green board fixed to the wall, and many single seats like in a real assembly room. It was his first time seeing an auditorium like this.

When the professor spoke, everybody quickly took notes, because he was so fast when speaking and projecting things on the screen. Gilbert felt left behind; he was not used to this fast tempo in high school. When he looked at the notes of his colleague sitting next to him, the guy told him, "Yeah, buddy, welcome to university!"

At the end of the day, when Gilbert got back home late, he was so tired and had already so many books to read and a lot of homework to do. He could not even eat well the food that his brother's fiancée, Mado, had cooked for them. Clearly, Gilbert was busier thinking about his homework than food.

When his brother came back home, he went straight to Gilbert's room. Gilbert was very busy reading and doing his homework. Henry asked him, "How was the first day in the department? And Mado told me you didn't really eat much food. Are you okay?"

Gilbert answered, "Nothing's wrong with me except they gave us a lot of homework on the first day. I think I will be okay after I get the rhythm in a few days."

Meanwhile, days were passing. Gilbert was missing his Monique and his parents in Pointe-Noire. He already sent two letters to Monique and one letter to his parents. But in those days, letters were taking two to three weeks before they got to their destination. It was typical to wait more than one month to get an answer from loved ones.

And because of his studies, he could not continue to write letters to Monique. In Brazzaville, Gilbert frequently met interesting girls in his department and others. These girls were beautiful too, and they were mature and intelligent like him. They could discuss many things in life. It was not the case with Monique, who had dropped out of high school. That was why, using this argument of having to wait a long time for Monique's letters and plenty of orthographic faults to come, Gilbert prefers just to keep silence. He wrote no more letters to Monique, even when she continued to send some.

Gilbert was more focused on his studies. If he wanted a girlfriend, he thought he would find one here instead of wasting time with a distant, unintellectual girl like Monique.

Chapter 5

In May, at the end of the academic year, Gilbert was among students who were selected by the Congo Education Ministry to continue their studies in different European countries. How did this happen?

One Saturday evening, when everybody was sitting at home listening to Radio Congo in Brazzaville, Gilbert and Henry were surprised to hear the name of Gilbert Mavinga cited among others by the radio speaker. This was a communication from the minister of education, asking selected first-year students from different departments of the University of Brazzaville to go on Monday to General Direction of Orientation and Scholarship for important information regarding their orientations.

On a very sunny day in May, most people were waiting for the retransmission of the football game via Radio Brazzaville. The Congo national team was going to play against the Black Stars of Ghana. So, it was likely that almost everybody in the city and in the country was listening to this communication and was already asking, "What could this be?"

But most well-informed people knew that when a student who was already attending university was called for orientation, it was generally for a scholarship. These students were most likely being offered a chance to continue their studies in Europe or even in well-organized North African countries.

Now, Gilbert and Henry turned their attention from the game to the news. They started asking many questions. Henry asked Gilbert, "If this is a scholarship to European universities, what country would you prefer?"

Gilbert answered, "I don't know. Maybe I would choose France because they speak French like us. I don't want to spend another year just to learn a new language. This would bring me one year back."

Would Gilbert get a scholarship to a European country like France?

At ten o'clock on Monday, when Gilbert arrived at General Direction of Orientation and Scholarship, he found many students like him who were already waiting to meet with the general director himself.

They called students one by one to the general director's office. Indeed, each student who came out of the general director's office had an offer to continue studies in another country. Most students were referred to Europe.

What about Gilbert? The general director told him he had been selected to continue his studies in Czechoslovakia. Right away Gilbert felt frustrated at the idea of going to a communistic East-European country. Back then, it was a shame for young students to go to communistic countries; they did not like it there. They preferred to go to Western countries. But the general director told him to feel happy because he himself studied psychology at University of Prague. And look at the position he was in now!

The general director's words convinced Gilbert to happily accept the scholarship to Czechoslovakia, where he was selected to study business management and accounting at University of Prague.

The trip to Prague was set for August 25. Globally, the General Direction of Orientation and Scholarship had two and a half months to prepare the passports, get airplane tickets, and pocket money for all traveling students.

In Gilbert's case, the General Direction had planned for him to go to Kinshasa in the DR Congo for a visa interview at the Czechoslovakia Embassy. He would be accompanied by an agent of the General Direction. There was no Czechoslovakia Embassy in Brazzaville, which was why they had to cross the border to Kinshasa for a visa.

Since Gilbert started preparing for his trip to Europe, things were going fast. After he got everything in his hands, his parents decided to come to Brazzaville to say good-bye to their son before he left for Czechoslovakia.

This was another honor set for the Mavinga family. "What a blessing for this family!" people were saying.

Monique knew that Gilbert was going to Czechoslovakia, but there was no way she could come to Brazzaville. She was no longer a priority for Gilbert, even though he still felt something for her.

Henry was so proud of his little brother and was helping him prepare for his trip to Europe. At nine o'clock at night, Gilbert would leave Brazzaville to go to Prague. But he must be at the airport two hours early for registration.

Gilbert wore a dark-blue three-piece suit for his trip to Prague. He had a red tie with dark-blue stripes and a sky-blue shirt. He looked sharp, like a diplomat.

At almost seven o'clock, the family left Henry's house. Gilbert was visibly nervous; his parents were too. Henry drove, and Gilbert sat next to him. Their parents sat in the backseat. Nobody was really talking because everything had already been said when they were home.

There were many people at Brazzaville International Airport, mostly students who were going to Europe like Gilbert. Gilbert would be taking a UTA flight to Paris. At that time, UTA was the principal company connecting most African countries with Europe. In this case, once passengers arrived in Paris, they were placed in different airplanes that were taking them to their final destinations in Europe.

The atmosphere at Brazzaville International Airport was electric. People were hugging and kissing each other and saying good-bye to their dear ones.

After Gilbert checked his luggage, he hugged his brother and father and then affectionately embraced his mother. He said, "I will see you again, Mother." This was a very moving moment in the life of the Mavinga family. Then he waved to them, entered the non-access zone, and disappeared inside the waiting room after he passed all immigration and customs checkpoints.

At exactly nine o'clock, UTA flight 54 to Paris was on the tarmac, ready for takeoff. The next minute, the airplane disappeared into the Brazzaville sky en route for Paris, where Gilbert would switch to a Czechoslovakia Airlines plane to go to Prague, his final destination.

Chapter 6

Gilbert slept the whole way to Europe. Even when the DC 10 Boeing 747 was crossing the space of the Sahara Desert or the Mediterranean Sea, Gilbert comfortably slept in his seat.

He woke up only at seven o'clock in the morning, when the pilot and commandant of the airplane said, "This is Captain Galant, pilot of the UTA DC 10 Boeing 747, flight 54 to Paris. In one minute, we will be landing in Nice Côte d'Azur International Airport for a two-hour technical stop. Please buckle your seat belts. Thank you."

And then he tilted the airplane to the left and right to give people a chance to see from the sky the city of Nice, on the border of the Mediterranean Sea. It was the most fabulous view Gilbert had ever seen. The Mediterranean Sea was all dark blue, and the city of Nice had buildings of medium height and well-landscaped green parks. The roads were well paved, with lights everywhere. This city looked like a painting drawn by a landscape artist.

On the ground, all the passengers going to Paris were pleased to not have to leave the airport but wait there for their next embarkation.

At this time of the day, it was cold outside. It seemed like most people in the city were still sleeping and did not want to wake up and go to work. Gilbert remembered a Congo song: *Africa moto, awa na Poto malili* ("Hot in Africa, but cold in Europe").

Gilbert quickly bought three beautiful cards and posted one to his brother Henry in Brazzaville, one to Monique, and one to his parents in Pointe-Noire. After the stop in Nice, all the passengers were pleased to get back onto their airplane and head to Paris. Gilbert used the two-and-half-hour flight from Nice to Paris as a long moment of contemplation of France's beautiful landscape. He fell in love with France. He said to himself, "If France is this beautiful, then God must certainly live in France!" Gilbert thought so just because he had never been anywhere else than his native Congo. This was his first time seeing something really different.

When the airplane touched down at Paris-Charles De Gaulle International Airport, it was eleven thirty. This was the must-exit stop, where passengers going to different countries were pleased to check in at the UTA information desk for the next flight to their final destination. When Gilbert got to the information desk, they told him to use the phone that was on the table and call the UTA Reservation Center to find out about his next flight to Prague. When Gilbert picked up the phone, he started imitating the real French accent. They told him he has already missed today's only flight to Prague. The next flight was the next day at eleven o'clock. But because it was not his fault, UTA would put him in a hotel near Paris-Orly International Airport. They told him to go to the fourth floor of the airport, where a shuttle bus would be waiting for him. It would take him to Sofitel Hotel. He would have a room at his disposal, lunch and dinner for today, plus a breakfast the next morning before the shuttle came at ten o'clock to take him back to Paris-Orly International Airport.

"A bus on the fourth floor? But I'm on the first floor. Where does it come from?" Gilbert asked himself.

A spirit inside him answered, "Oh yes, my man, this is Paris and you haven't seen anything yet."

When he took the elevator to the fourth floor, he was surprised to see that the fourth floor was at ground level, like the first floor. He didn't know that the building was mounted on a fake four-story slope.

At the fourth floor UTA desk, he asked, "Is this the floor where I'm supposed to get my shuttle to Sofitel Hotel?"

And the white lady at the desk answered, "Are you the person who just talked to me on the phone about going to Prague tomorrow?"

"Yes, it's me," answered Gilbert.

Then the lady said, "I am really impressed. I thought you were a native Frenchman talking to me with a real French accent, but I see you must come from black Africa and certainly from the Congo, isn't it?"

"Yes, I am a real black man from Congo who's never been to Europe before," said Gilbert.

The lady added, "Your French is perfect, and you're just a charming young man!"

"Thank you, madam," answered Gilbert.

The lady said finally, "Your bus is right outside. The driver is waiting for you."

After he placed his luggage in his hotel room, he went straight to the restaurant. At the table the waitress asked him what he wanted to eat. Gilbert did not have any clue about names of the meals in French, even when he was holding the menu that contained all the names of the meals. But it was understandable, because he had never been in a restaurant like this before. So he did his best to quickly choose a meal because the waitress was pressing him to make his choice. She had many other tables to serve. Then he shouted, "I want an omelet." This was the only word he recognized on the menu. He could not tell how the other meals in the menu looked and tasted.

The waitress asked, *Vous voulez une omelette aux allumettes?* ("You want an omelet with small-cut French fries?")

He said, *Einh?*

The waitress thought he said, "Yes," and left.

Gilbert didn't know that *omelette aux allumettes* meant "omelet with French fries cut very small like matchsticks." He did not want to take the risk of ordering another kind of dish because he did not want to look ridiculous eating something he'd never tried before. At least he knew what omelet meant and what the matchsticks were. So he would eat the omelet with bread that was already on his table and leave the matchsticks alone.

Out of the corner of his eyes he looked at the food that other people were eating. Some of them were having good-looking dishes from which he could easily recognize a well-fried chicken breast or leg, but he could not order that because he didn't know its French name on the menu.

When the waitress came back with the omelet dish he had ordered, he discovered that *allumettes* were simply French fries cut very small, not matchsticks. Now he was assured and regained his little smile.

The next morning Gilbert was on his Czechoslovakia Airlines flight. The flight attendants were tall, blonde, and beautiful, and they were all smiling. They spoke a little English but not enough to flirt with.

At about eleven forty-five in the morning, the Soviet Union aircraft model *Tupolev* took off for Prague, the capital city of Czechoslovakia. The flight was smooth, and once again Gilbert had time to contemplate by daylight the European landscape.

"It is beautiful here," he said.

But the more east they were going, the colder the temperature was becoming. The temperature was below fifteen degrees centigrade, which was already cold for Gilbert.

After two hours the airplane got into Prague's airspace, and the pilot started a complete round of the city. He said, "This is Captain Buzasky of flight 842 to Prague. We have started our descent to Prague International Airport. We are landing in three minutes. All passengers are pleased to stay in their seats and buckle their seat belts. Thank you."

From sky, the city of Prague looked so beautiful—even more beautiful than Paris. The buildings, the roads, and the parks all looked splendid. And Gilbert couldn't hide his joy to finally arrive in Prague.

At exactly two o'clock in the evening, the Tupolev finally landed on the tarmac of Prague International Airport.

After twenty minutes, Gilbert was outside the airport checkpoints and was already asking for information about how to get to the students' village of the University of Prague. He had all the information on the paper he got from the Czechoslovakia Embassy in Kinshasa, but he preferred to ask to get confirmation.

He was surprised to see a black man approaching him. This one looked young, around twenty-five. The man said in French to Gilbert, *Bonjour Monsieur; je m'appelle Paul Mountou du Congo et vous êtes certainement Gilbert Mavinga du Congo?* ("Hello, sir. My name is Paul Mountou of the Congo, and you are probably Gilbert Mavinga from the Congo?")

Gilbert was so relieved to see a black man here, where it was practically impossible to meet one. Not only did he speak French, but he was from the Congo too. At first look, Gilbert thought Paul worked for the Congo Embassy in Prague. But he was wrong. Back then Congo did not have an embassy in Prague. Paul was a finalist of the department of economy at University of Prague. As a longtime Congo student here, the dean of the department had informed him about a new Congo student who was coming to study in their department. So he was so happy when they asked him to go pick him up at the airport on the day of his arrival.

Paul was not alone. There were three other Congo students waiting for him outside of the airport. Everybody greeted him fraternally and told him, "Welcome to Prague, Gilbert."

He answered, "This is a nice surprise for me to meet with my compatriots on my first day in Prague. Thank you, guys, for your patriotism and your sympathy."

Nobody had their own car. They opted for public transportation, which worked well here. For the first time, Gilbert could sit in a tramway and ride from the airport straight to the students' village of the University of Prague.

At the students' village, Gilbert was set to live with Paul in a two-room apartment. They had to share one toilet and a shower. Their apartment was on the second floor of the building. On each floor, all students had one large kitchen with many electric plates, where they could cook whatever they wanted. To do their laundry, all students in the building had to get the key to the laundry room from the concierge and go to the basement, where all the washing machines were located.

Right next to their building was a small farm with many apple trees. From his window in his room, Gilbert could see outside and, for the first time, see a farm with apple trees.

On his first night, Gilbert did not know how to use all the bedcovers at his disposal. He had a duvet cover, a duvet itself, a pillow and its covers, and a couple of sheets. So he covered the bed with the sheets and put the duvet on the bed, because he thought the duvet was there to be put on the bed for more comfort during sleep. Also, he did not think to cover the pillow with the pillowcase. He took the duvet cover, slipped into it like into a sleeping bag, and went to sleep.

The next day, Paul knocked on his door and asked how he spent the first night. Gilbert quickly opened the door, and Paul could immediately see that Gilbert was not covering the duvet. He asked Gilbert, "How did you use your duvet?"

Gilbert answered, "What's a duvet?"

Paul went to Gilbert's bed and showed him the duvet.

Gilbert said, "I put it on the bed, and because it was so cold, I slipped into this double sheet that looks like an envelope."

When Paul heard what Gilbert just said, he started laughing and said to Gilbert, "No, buddy, the thing you put on the bed is called a duvet. You should put it in the double sheet you call an envelope and then cover your body with it. Also, the small envelope you have left aside is used to cover your pillow."

Both laughed for almost half an hour.

At the Czech Language Institute at University of Prague, Gilbert had a very busy schedule. In his first year, he had to learn the Czech language. In the first three months he would take an intensive course of Czech language only. After the first three months, he would take other scientific courses. This way he would have command of the Czech language, which would help him in his studies the next year at university.

The Czech language labs were well equipped, and only the most talented and professional teachers were in charge of teaching foreign students here. Students from all around the world were set in groups depending on their major. For example, students who were going to study economics were put in same economics groups. The same thing went for students who would study medicine, chemistry, engineering, and more.

Students from different countries attended the Institute of Czech Language, including African countries (like Congo, Gabon, Cameroon, Nigeria, Senegal, Ghana, Zambia, Angola, Namibia, Lesotho, Kenya, Algeria, Tunisia, Libya, Egypt, Ethiopia, etc.), European countries (like Albania, Romania, Hungary, East Germany, Poland, Greece, Turkey, Yugoslavia, Soviet Union, etc.), Middle East and Asian countries (like Palestine, Iran, Iraq, Mongolia, Vietnam, Bangladesh, India, Pakistan, North Korea, China, etc.), and South and Central American countries (like Mexico, Cuba, Panama, Honduras, Peru, Chile, Brazil, Venezuela, Argentina, Bolivia, Colombia, etc.).

For the first time in his life Gilbert could sit in the same classroom with students from Greece, Namibia, India,

Mexico, Panama, Chile, and Vietnam and have Czech teachers as mentors. This was fabulous because in Prague Gilbert was becoming an international student from the Congo. With his new friends from different countries, Gilbert could play soccer with them and, more importantly, learn about each other's culture.

Meanwhile, Gilbert continued to keep in touch with his family. He received letters from his parents and his girlfriend, Monique, in Pointe-Noire and also from his brother Henry in Brazzaville. The letters took about three weeks to arrive. So, on average, he received one or two letters every month and a half. And he could immediately answer his letters even when his schedule was so busy.

One time his father put the wrong address on the envelope. He wrote Gilbert's address right, but he added the word "France" at the end of the name of the country, Czechoslovakia. This additional word made this letter go first to France and then finally to the true destination after more than two months. All this happened because of the influence of the French colony. Years ago, Congo was a French colony. Since then, almost every old man in Congo thought that going to Europe meant going to France. They didn't know anything about countries other than France.

During this time in Eastern Europe, people's living situations became worse in most countries that were under the Soviet Union supremacy. In Czechoslovakia and in Poland the voices of leaders like Vaclav Havel and Lech Walesa could be heard, with the support of all people behind them. Mikhail Gorbachev was already talking about *perestroika* and *glasnost*. President Ronald Regan was pushing people to freedom and real democracy. And the intention of breaking the wall separating the two Berlins was becoming loud.

A social explosion would occur soon in these countries where people, living in inhumane conditions, could not take it anymore. This was the case in Poland, Czechoslovakia, Romania, Bulgaria, and even East Germany, where meat and bread were rationed. This was a very tough period for these countries after World War II.

In the rural areas of these countries, people were completely lost and had almost no connection with the outside world. When they saw a black man walking on the street they thought he had black paint on his skin to look like a clown. The way these regimes restricted people from news made them look like cave people that had never seen civilization before. They didn't want them to discover the reality of the world, and they were scared that people would understand what was wrong and soon would go to the streets and protest.

Chapter 7

Since Gilbert had passed with distinction his first year of language learning, he had also finished his first year. Now he was in his second year of economics at University of Prague. His compatriot Paul Mountou had already finished his studies and had returned to Congo.

For each Congo student who spent three years overseas, the Congo government would send a ticket for him to take a vacation and go back to Congo. This was the case for Gilbert. Immediately after he finished his second year of economics at University of Prague, he was lucky to get his airplane ticket and take his first vacation in Congo.

With the money he was getting every month from the Congo government, Gilbert managed to buy some good stuff in diplomatic shops called *Tuzex*, which were reserved for foreigners. This way he avoided going to West Berlin, Germany, or to France, where most Congo students used to go for shopping before they made the trip back to Congo. In diplomatic shops people could find all the best things they could not buy in the Czech market. Only foreigners with foreign money or some privileged Czech people who had a chance to buy foreign money at their own risk in the black market could buy things here. Except the *Tuzex*, people in Czechoslovakia did not have a place where they could buy really good things. In local stores the only good things that could be found were some caveman fur coats, some Santa Claus shoes, and other archaic clothes. Sometimes when people were lucky, they could get into a store that had been newly supplied, but still they had to stand in long lines and also possess a ration card to buy a pair of shoes, a shirt, or a pair of underwear.

This was a daily reality show in the life of the people in this part of the world. It was like a romantic period that no one could forget.

Before leaving Prague to go to Congo for vacation, Gilbert did his best to pass all his exams on time. He had bought a lot of presents for his family and friends in Congo. Gilbert went directly to Pointe-Noire to visit his parents and also to see his girlfriend, from whom he hadn't received any news for a long time.

In Pointe-Noire, emotions were very high when he saw people he had left four years ago. Everybody looked at him very differently and approached him with a lot of respect. The man had changed in every way. He looked more mature, grown, and healthy compared to other people his age.

When Congo people living in Europe went back to Congo for vacation, they had to show an improvement in class with the way they dressed, walked, and looked. It was a tradition. Everybody in the area would talk about them, their clothes, and the way they walked and talked. They become icons, models that people would imitate. It was a privilege for the Mavinga family to have such a wonderful boy—intelligent, well dressed, and rich because he already had a future.

Gilbert's mother and father were examples for others in the society; they both had one very successful son Henry in Brazzaville, and another one was studying in Europe and had in front of him a bright future. Each family wished to be like them. And Gilbert and his family were just becoming the heroes for many people in Pointe-Noire.

While everything was going well, something was missing. Where was Monique? Monique could not show up in front of Gilbert. Gilbert's mother told Gilbert about what happened to Monique. She said Monique could not wait any longer for Gilbert's letters, which were taking a long time to get to her. Some of them even went missing. Also, four years without seeing each other was the factor that allowed Monique to decide to go with another man. She had a new fiancé who had proposed to her and was getting ready to marry her. And when Gilbert's mother told the story, Monique was already living in her fiancé's house. This was the tradition; a young man and his family made the first proposal to the girl's family about marrying their daughter. From then on, he had the right to go with his future wife and live with her until the day he was ready to finally marry his wife.

With this news, Gilbert was sure that his relationship with Monique was over.

After two months well spent in Congo, mostly in Pointe-Noire, Gilbert returned to Prague. He had to be ready for the beginning of his third year at University of Prague.

Many of his Congolese, Czech, and other friends asked him how he spent his vacation time in Congo. He had brought some Congo dried and frozen foods and other stuff from the Congo. He tried to explain to his friends how all these things were used in Congo. For his Congo brothers (the Congo students in Prague), he had already set up a typical Congo meal that Gilbert was going to cook. The food would be composed of crushed cassava leaves cooked with fish inside, mixed with an eggplant and other condiments. All would be partially fried in palm oil. This well-done meal would be accompanied by steamed white rice and fried fish, like round scad or red snapper. Voilà! Bon appétit!

For Congo students, this was also a way to meet together and gather information about the country. Everybody wanted to know what had changed in the Congo since they left. They talked about almost everything: the political life in Congo, the music and new dances, sports (mostly soccer), the sanitation situation in the cities like Pointe-Noire and Brazzaville, and the social life of the population.

The next day was the beginning of the new academic year at the University of Prague. Gilbert started his third year in economics pretty well. He had a good schedule, and he thought he would have more time to go to the library for research. He felt more motivated since he came back from the Congo.

He didn't care about losing Monique. He cared about finishing his studies and going back to Congo, getting a good job, and helping his family. Getting married was the last thing he cared about. He knew that with a good situation in life, girls would be drawn to him like flies. He would then make a decent choice. For now he would focus on his studies.

This academic year quickly came to the end. This time it was easy for Gilbert. The more he continued his studies, the more he felt comfortable with the Czech language and the study of business management at University of Prague.

In the upcoming academic year Gilbert would really get deep into his specialization in business management and accounting.

Chapter 8

In a different country, the Democratic Republic of Congo, lived two families in the capital city Kinshasa: the Tshiputus and the Kasusus. Both families lived here for a long time, next to each other in the same area of the city.

Mr. Marcel Tshiputu was married to Ma-Sangi Tshiputu, and they had one sixteen-year-old girl, Dorothy, and three younger boys. Mr. Marcel Tshiputu was a high-ranking government official. He worked in the Ministry of Foreign Affairs, where he had the privilege of being in charge of the Division of Bilateral Exchanges and Cooperation. He was a very influential and respected man. He dealt only with high-ranking people like himself. He talked directly to his boss, the minister of foreign affairs, without an intermediary.

For his job, he was equipped with an official and luxurious car, and he had all the privileges due to a person of his rank. The house he lived in with his family was built with his own money accumulated from advantages related to his position, but not really from his salary.

In this country everybody knew that nobody could afford to build a beautiful house or buy a luxurious car with his official salary. People knew that when you were lucky to get a job, you must do your best to take advantage of your post and quickly build your life. If you had to steal, you must do it as fast as possible, before the guy who helped you get to this position got discharged and replaced by another.

Justice existed in this country but would never be applied to someone who had already acquired so much money by stealing directly from the government, using all the tricks in his possession. Here, when you had money, nobody touched you. Government was completely corrupt. There was no other place in the world where a high-ranking army general could go to a foreign businessman (mostly Lebanese) and ask him to give him money in exchange for service. The army general would protect him any time he had problems with the tax collection services or any other kind of problems. He would send an entire army brigade to protect this criminal, just because he needed money to live better with his family. He was ready to kill his own people to protect the guys who made his country miserable for people living there. And the army general had strong connections within the government.

Most foreign businessmen in the DR Congo could do anything they wanted and never be punished by the law. They could quickly put money on the table to corrupt anybody who stood in their way. Anybody who tried to resist them would have to answer to the army general or other high-ranking officials. Of course, guys like these could easily end up in jail for trying to distract a foreign contractor who was conducting his business to help the country's economy grow. That was why even African businesspeople who were dealing in the DR Congo did the same things that other foreigners did.

One day in Kinshasa, a Senegalese businessman who managed a small grocery store got mad at tax collection agents who came to verify and discuss the tax documents he hadn't filed properly. He told them directly, "I don't want to see you any longer in my store. I ask you to leave this place; otherwise I call the general."

One of the agents asked, "What will a general do here? We are not at war."

He responded, "The general's people will beat you up and arrest you for distracting me in my job."

"But our job is to verify tax documents," said another agent.

Then, this Senegalese guy called the general, who said he was sending a brigade to get these agents. The agents decided to leave, because they knew it was not a joke. The general's people would really do what he asked them to do. So it was better to go and protect their lives.

When they left, the army brigade arrived but did not find anybody. They told the Senegalese businessman, "Do not worry! We will try to find them and put them all in jail if we get them." And the Senegalese man gave a ten-dollar bill to each army guy before they left his store.

People passing by were visibly afraid and astonished. They were just standing and watching the situation from a distance.

After the army brigade left, the Senegalese man said, *Congo zoba ah ah* ("Congo people are stupid ah ah"). Congolese people who heard these words were so mad and frustrated, but there was not much they could do to this guy, who they said looked as dark as charcoal.

Mr. Marcel Tshiputu had put all his children in very good schools. Dorothy attended a private high school in downtown Kinshasa. This was a very prestigious school where only children from well-established families went. Curiously, Dorothy attended the same school as her friend Thomas Kasusu, who was the first son of their neighbors. Dorothy was in ninth grade, and Thomas was in twelfth grade. Students in their final year were called finalists, because at the end of the year they would pass the very prestigious high school final exam called *Examen d'Etat*.

Mr. Gabriel Kasusu was the head of the Kasusu family. He was married to Ma-Marie Kasusu. They had five children, and Tomas was the elder son.

Mr. Gabriel Kasusu worked in the private sector of the import-export business. Generally, he used to import goods from Asian countries to the DR Congo. He always traveled to Asian countries, mostly to China, to buy things like rice, wheat flour, sugar, dried and salted fish, tea, construction equipment, various materials, and tools. He put all the merchandise he bought in large containers and then shipped them from any open port in Asia via maritime ways to the DR Congo Port of Matadi. The merchandise took three to four weeks to get to Matadi. When he paid all the fees related to this activity, the containers were put on the tracks and were taken to Kinshasa by train.

Mr. Gabriel Kasusu bought everything in Asia very cheaply. The maritime transportation was not expensive. And given the corruption in the DR Congo, Mr. Gabriel Kasusu knew very well how to deal with all the services in the Port of Matadi.

Corruption in the Port of Matadi was the highest in the country. All imported merchandise that filled the DR Congo market arrived via the maritime way. And ipso facto, the Port of Matadi had become a place for personal enrichment. All government agencies that worked here included plenty of highly corrupt people. They did not think of bringing money to the public treasury, but they built a nice life for their families. That was why so many beautiful houses and cars, which typical DR Congo people could not afford, crowded the city of Matadi. It seemed that everyone here was rich, but really everyone was a thief.

People with the regular government salary—a port service agent working for the Congo Office of Control, the National Office of Transportation, the customs office, and other service—could not afford to acquire all these houses and cars and maintain this kind of life. They all were corrupt. The corruption was a chain, going from a simple agent to the director in charge of the service. They even had connections with the main offices in Kinshasa.

To avoid getting audited, the bosses of local agencies in the Port of Matadi were directly in touch with the highest cadres in Kinshasa who were able to send a complacent audit service that would close their eyes on any wrongdoing they found in Matadi. The audit service agents were corrupt, as well. This way nobody knew anything, and nobody said anything to anybody. The corruption was generalized and institutionalized.

Once Mr. Gabriel Kasusu's merchandise had passed all the corrupt stages on the way to Kinshasa, he could finally recoup his merchandise, stock it nicely, and then sell it at a very high price. Nobody would control his retail prices because he knew all the people and all the tricks.

Mr. Gabriel Kasusu was also considered a very wealthy man in the city. That was why there was a big rivalry between the Tshiputu family and the Kasusu family. This was the way things worked here in the DR Congo. And because of their rivalry, living side by side had become difficult for these two families. If one family bought a new car, the other family did its best to buy a new car too. The members of both families clashed almost every day.

In the meantime, Dorothy Tshiputu and Thomas Kasusu attended the same school and saw each other and talked nicely every day. They may have even been intimate. They liked each other very much. But when Dorothy was home, her mother always told her not to talk to Thomas—not even to try.

Thomas's mother told him the same thing. One day she said to Thomas, "I do not want you to talk to that fat girl at school. She is not your type and will never be your type. You know we don't like her mom. She is always provocative with our family."

Chapter 9

The parents of Thomas and Dorothy could say whatever they wanted, but they could not stop their children from continuing to see each other at school or even at some corners in the city.

Thomas Kasusu, nineteen, looked awesome. He was tall, with a long face and small growing beard on his chin. His eyes were small and narrow, like those of a Japanese boy. His skin was very clean and was a chocolate-brown color. He was very beautiful for a boy his age. This was what made girls his age, including Dorothy Tshiputu, run after him.

Dorothy Tshiputu, sixteen, was a very charming girl. She was not skinny, but her body was curvy, and she had a nicely formed backside. She had beautiful round eyes, and nobody passed her without turning their head to look at her a second time. Her tight pants or skirts always looked sexy on her, and boys went crazy when she walked down the street.

What their parents did not want to happen was exactly what happened. Thomas and Dorothy became boyfriend and girlfriend. At the beginning, nobody knew about their relationship. They tried to hide it, but people were able to find out about it. A Congo song in Lingala says, *Amour ya kobombama, soki bolingo eleki, ekosuka kaka mama, bato nionso bakoyeba* ("You might hide your love in front of people, but somehow people will still know about it"). That was what happened in this case.

One day, while Thomas was in the *Maquis* (a private house that people rent for their children to stay for a few weeks to study for their final high school exam), Dorothy decided to visit him. She brought all kinds of candies and canned foods for Thomas. One thing she didn't know was that her mom was suspicious. When Dorothy told her that she was going to visit her aunt who lived in another area of the city, her mom did a tricky thing. She followed Dorothy one hour after she left. But when Dorothy's mother got to her sister's house, there was no sign of Dorothy there. She waited long enough and finally decided to follow Dorothy to the place where she was told by her own "informers" that Thomas was staying to study for his final high school exam.

Then the big clash started when she saw Thomas and Dorothy sitting together in the *Maquis* house. Thomas's friends witnessed the event.

Dorothy's mother started yelling, "Hey, you! Who told you to stay with my daughter? You ugly boy, look at your head, like a traditional charcoal iron. How dare you be with my daughter? I will have a serious talk with your mama today. She will know who I am. And the next time I see you with my daughter, I will get you arrested for going with a minor."

Nobody answered to her.

In Congo, everybody knew that kids of this age were almost uncontrollable. They did things that even grown people couldn't do. They were unpredictable. That made Dorothy's mother crazy.

She turned to Dorothy and said, "You lied to me. I went to your aunt's, but you were not there. You are here, wasting your time with this Casanova. Come right now and let's go back home." Then she took her to her car and left.

Back home the scene was insane. Dorothy's mother started to yell at Thomas's mother. "You woman, watch after your child. If I find him going with my Dorothy again, I will get him arrested. Instead of studying for his final exam, he keeps rocking my daughter around with his big flat head."

Right away Thomas's mother answered, "Shut up, you ugly mama. Leave my Thomas alone. It's your fat girl who is running after my boy. He doesn't want her. She is not his type."

The quarrel took place on the street, and everybody was watching them yell at each other.

"This is a shame for people of your rank to quarrel like this in the middle of the street," said an onlooker.

But the two women didn't care and continued to exchange harsh words. They were almost about to physically fight, but people stopped them by sending them to their respective houses.

Days passed. Thomas and Dorothy did not care about what their parents were saying. Their love was becoming even crazier; and the clashes between their parents intensified every time they saw them walking together.

But in the middle of this, Thomas had managed to graduate from high school with honors. He scored 70 percent in the final exam, and he was accepted to study at the University of Kinshasa, where he planned to study finance in the department of economics.

In the meantime, he continued to live underground with his girlfriend, Dorothy. They were so much in love that nothing could stop them.

After three years, when Thomas was twenty-two and was in his third year of economics, Dorothy graduated from high school with 60 percent. She was now nineteen.

This was the perfect moment for which Dorothy's mother and father were waiting to act. For a long time now, Dorothy's father had arranged a scholarship for his daughter. They planned to send her overseas to continue her studies. They had arranged everything for Dorothy. She could go to Czechoslovakia and pursue her studies at University of Prague.

This way, they were sure to separate her from Thomas and forever end their relationship.

Dorothy's parents told their daughter about this. "You know, you will love studying there. The country is very beautiful, and people are very nice," they said to her.

For Dorothy's parents, this was the best present they could give to their daughter after her high school graduation. And Dorothy didn't have the option to refuse. She had to agree with her parents' decision to go to Europe for studies and get separated from her lovely boyfriend. So, in front of her parents, she faked being very happy about going to Czechoslovakia.

Meanwhile, when she met with her boyfriend and told him about this news, he went crazy. They both cried. But the two accomplices got an idea. They decided to have a baby before she left for Europe. This was something that would surprise both parents on both sides.

Then Thomas got Dorothy pregnant, and nobody knew about it. The pregnancy would be visible after a few months, when Dorothy would be in Czechoslovakia.

Just a month after this happened, Dorothy was about to leave Kinshasa to go to Prague. It was the middle of August, and she and Thomas were keeping their secret to themselves. And to make things easy, both Dorothy and Thomas decided to suddenly change their behavior in front of their respective parents. They started acting very nicely when talking to their parents, and they did everything in their power to not let their parents see them walking together. But deep in their hearts, they knew very well what they had already done. That would be a big surprise, like a bomb exploding in the near future.

At N'djili Airport in Kinshasa, Dorothy was with her parents and one of her younger brothers. In few moments she would leave Kinshasa, but clearly she was not really sad to leave her boyfriend, Thomas. She knew she had another little Thomas inside of her, so she didn't care about what her parents had planned.

After all the formalities at N'djili Airport in Kinshasa, she disappeared inside the waiting room. Her mother and father waited until the airplane took off before leaving the airport and returning home. Joy was visible on the faces of Dorothy's mother and father. Clearly they felt satisfied, having separated Dorothy from Thomas.

Air Sabena would take Dorothy directly to Brussels, the capital city of Belgium, where she was going to switch to Czechoslovakia Airlines to go to Prague.

Chapter 10

The next day, after she left Kinshasa, Dorothy arrived in Prague. Gilbert was the first person she met in Prague. Gilbert, who was a citizen of the Congo Republic, was charged by his department to go to the airport and help Dorothy Tshiputu, a new student from the Democratic Republic of Congo, come to Prague to study economics at University of Prague. The department staff did not have DR Congo students studying economics; that was why they just picked up Gilbert, who was from neighboring Congo Republic to help them in this. The DR Congo students in Prague were mostly studying in other departments or were attending different universities.

For Gilbert, this was a pretty nice assignment and a privilege. When a new African girl was coming to the department, all the African boys were on maximum alert. Clearly, they wanted to have a girlfriend from their native continent. They felt more comfortable living with their own Mandingo girl than with a white Czech girl.

That was why, when Gilbert got the news, he didn't want all his African friends to know about it, especially those from the Congo. Gilbert thought they would become serious contenders, and his chances to get Dorothy's heart would become slim.

Gilbert got this news in the middle of August, just when he was getting ready to start the upcoming academic year. And that day at the Prague International Airport, when Gilbert met with Dorothy Tshiputu, he said in his heart, "Finally, this is my very charming girl I have always dreamed of." He was very excited to meet her. He knew she would be studying economics in the same department as him.

People from the Congo Republic and the Democratic Republic of Congo were very similar. They had the same dialects and spoke the same official language (French)—even when the countries were colonized by two different European countries, France and Belgium. The capital cities of both countries were next to each other, separated only by the Congo River, which could be crossed by ferryboat in fifteen minutes.

Gilbert saw Dorothy, and they talked in French. He knew immediately that something was happening right there. His heart started beating very fast, and the connection was there. Without hesitation this was love at first sight.

Gilbert was very agitated in helping her with all the formalities at the Institute of Czech Language. After her first year here, she would be attending the department of economics, where Gilbert was studying.

Gilbert was becoming the man in charge of Dorothy. He didn't let anybody get close to her. Clearly Gilbert was already in love with this girl. Instinctively, she felt something for him too, but she kept cool and calm, like all the girls did.

Dorothy was put in a two-room apartment, where she had another African girl from Kenya as a neighbor. Dorothy was happy to have her as a neighbor, because the girl from Kenya spoke Swahili, and Dorothy spoke Swahili too. Dorothy's family was originally from the southeastern part of the DR Congo, where people spoke Swahili. Kenya natives knew very well the DR Congo people. They liked the Congo music, which was very popular in Africa and Europe.

Days and months were passed by fast, and by the time other African boys got the news of the new girl who came from the DR Congo, Gilbert and Dorothy were already living as boyfriend and girlfriend. They were already in love. While living together as boyfriend and girlfriend, Dorothy and Gilbert decided to open up to each other. Gilbert told Dorothy everything about his previous love life, but there really wasn't much of one.

Dorothy also told Gilbert everything. She told him that in Kinshasa she had a boyfriend she loved very much. But now that she met Gilbert, she didn't care anymore about the boyfriend in Kinshasa. Also, she said that just before leaving Kinshasa, she got pregnant with his child. She told Gilbert that she didn't know what to do now that she was in love with Gilbert. But one thing she knew for sure was that she would never take the risk of aborting her first child. It was now up to Gilbert to accept (or not accept) the situation.

It was obvious Gilbert was in trouble, but he did not care. As long as he and Dorothy were in love, nothing could stop him from living with her.

After five months, Dorothy's pregnancy became evident. In the meantime, Dorothy wrote a letter to her parents to let them know she was pregnant with Thomas

Kasusu's child. The news was so serious that her mother fell in a little depression. She was taken to the hospital in Kinshasa, treated, and released after one week. When she came back home, it was a huge scandal for the Kasusu family, especially for their son Thomas.

But whatever she could say would not change anything. The worst was already done. Now they had to deal with the situation. The Congo proverb said, "The palm wine is extracted; now let's drink it."

But Dorothy's mother was not done yet. She asked her husband, who had strong connections in the ministry of foreign affairs, to get all necessary documents for her so she could travel in three months to Prague. She planned to go there to assist her daughter during accouchement and also take the newborn baby back to the DR Congo. This way, her daughter would be free and could study without troubles.

Dorothy did not have any clue about this new plan. Even her boyfriend, Thomas Kasusu, did not have information about this.

Then, in the eighth month of Dorothy's pregnancy, Dorothy got an unexpected surprise from her mother, who arrived in Prague. Dorothy and Gilbert could not believe that Dorothy's mother had come to Prague to assist her daughter in her last days before giving birth.

Dorothy introduced Gilbert to her mother. "Mammy, please meet Gilbert, my boyfriend. We are both deeply in love. I told him about my pregnancy, and we both have accepted to keep my baby. He promised me to be a good dad for my baby, and we are planning to get married in the near future."

Gilbert said, "Very nice to meet you, Ma-Sangi."

She asked, "Are you really accepting my daughter with her upcoming baby?"

"Of course, yes. It's like she said," answered Gilbert.

Dorothy's mother was so visibly moved by Gilbert's dexterity and class. Dorothy's mother stayed with her daughter in her room, and Gilbert came to visit them both daily and also to see how Dorothy's baby was doing in its mother's belly. This way, Dorothy's mother had almost forgotten about the "ugly" Thomas Kasusu in Kinshasa. She convinced Dorothy that she was taking her baby to Kinshasa to leave her alone and free for studies. She said that if Dorothy kept the baby with her in Prague, she would not have time for both studies and caring for the baby.

Dorothy accepted because she knew that she would be free to enjoy time with Gilbert. She also knew that the final page with Thomas Kasusu will have been turned over. And clearly, her mother preferred Gilbert to Thomas.

Finally, in the ninth month of her pregnancy, Dorothy gave birth to a baby girl. Everybody was very happy to see the newborn baby. Dorothy named her baby girl Nisha. Baby Nisha was adorable, with her tiny face, tiny feet, and tiny hands. She looked just like her mother. She had clear skin, a small mouth, and small round eyes.

But the joy would last just for one month, because Dorothy's mother was taking baby Nisha to Kinshasa, after signing all the administrative and medical agreements and certifications. It was very sad for Dorothy to let her little baby Nisha go to Kinshasa with her grandmother. She was already getting used to her baby. But her mother was very clever. She did not want Dorothy to get too attached to the baby; instead, she was the one to do everything for the baby. She was in charge of feeding Nisha her baby formula and changing her diapers. This way, baby Nisha would think that Dorothy's mother was her real mother, not Dorothy.

When the day came that Dorothy's mother was leaving Prague with baby Nisha, Dorothy cried. Gilbert was the one who calmed her down. Dorothy did not want to go to the airport, but Gilbert did out of respect for his fiancée's mother.

At four o'clock in the evening, Gilbert and Dorothy's mother, along with baby Nisha, were at Prague International Airport. Baby Nisha was calm and slept the whole time. After almost one hour, Gilbert had a chance to see how the iron lady would embark on the airplane with a one-and-a-half-month-old baby, born from her daughter Dorothy. After a few more minutes, the Czechoslovakia Airlines airplane took off and disappeared in the sky of Prague. Baby Nisha and her iron grandmother left Prague en route for Kinshasa via Brussels.

Chapter 11

In Kinshasa, the life of little Nisha was going well. Nisha was completely attached to her grandmother because of the decent and fair care she was getting from her on a daily basis. She probably thought that Ma-Sangi was her birth mother. That was why she felt very comfortable with her grandmother Ma-Sangi. This confidence between them helped little Nisha grow fast and strong.

At the same time, Dorothy Tshiputu in Prague was impatient, waiting for news of her daughter from the DR Congo. But the time it took for letters to arrive was driving Dorothy crazy. She had to wait a long time before she could get a new photo of her little girl or any news about her. At least she was confident that she would see her when the time came. She knew very well that she was not allowed to go back to Kinshasa now, because nobody could predict what might happen if she met up with Thomas Kasusu. That was why her parents asked her to stay calm alone, without a baby and far away from Thomas Kasusu. This way she could study calmly and succeed in her studies.

So for now, the only thing she could enjoy was the moment when she got a letter from the DR Congo with photos of her daughter inside. And she enjoyed being in Gilbert's company. He always made her forget about her problems.

Back in Kinshasa, the situation was becoming a little confused between Nisha's families. Dorothy's mother didn't want the Kasusu family to see their granddaughter. She just chose to be mean to them. She wanted to take her revenge on them, saying that if they needed to see their granddaughter they should have gone to Prague like she did.

After many discussions and negotiations led by good people in their area, the Tshiputu family agreed to let Thomas Kasusu and his family see their little girl too. They even gave them two days a week to take little Nisha to their house.

This was a very big victory and a joyful moment for the Kasusu family, because it was not easy after many months to get a chance to see and take home their little girl too.

Two years passed, and Dorothy hadn't physically met again with her two-year-old girl. Dorothy had finished her first year of business management at University of Prague. Gilbert was very helpful in her success too.

At the same time, the political situation in the country where Gilbert and Dorothy were studying had changed. The people of Czechoslovakia had finally liberated themselves from the Soviet Empire. The country had gone through separatist conflict that led peacefully to the division of the Czechoslovakia Republic into two countries: the Czech Republic and Slovakia.

Little Nisha in Kinshasa was doing very well. She had two grandmothers and two grandfathers, plus a very loving dad. Every day, she spent her time in both houses built next to each other. But Dorothy's mother had more authority of little Nisha. She was the one who decided what to do with Nisha each day. Nisha must have been having fun. She was treated like a princess by both her families, and she seemed to enjoy her life.

When one grandmother bought her a dress, the other grandmother bought her a dress too. The same thing went for candies and others sweets. The small girl was really adored and was very intelligent for her age too.

⊷══◉◉══⊷

Meanwhile, many things in Thomas Kasusu's life had changed. Since Dorothy left, Thomas had done his best to completely finish the five years of finance studies at University of Kinshasa. He now had a master's degree in economic sciences with specialization in finances.

Immediately after he graduated from University of Kinshasa, Thomas Kasusu's father used his strong business connections with top administrators of OFIDA to get his son Thomas hired by OFIDA. With this job, Thomas's life was intense. He was making much money and had many girlfriends running after him. He did not care about Dorothy anymore, except that they had a fast-growing little girl together.

Working as a controller for OFIDA was the most wanted job of every young graduate in the DR Congo. This was because controllers were the ones who sealed the deals with clients. And to avoid paying much money to the Congo customs services for imported merchandise, clients were always ready to corrupt the controller who was in charge of their merchandise. The controller also had to secure his deals by giving away a part of his corrupt money to his high-ranking bosses. If he was happy, they were happy too. This forever maintained the corruption in this country.

This was why OFIDA agents made much more money than people working in other poor governmental departments like education, health, and social work. They possessed beautiful cars and houses and had better lives than anybody else in the cities where they operated. An OFIDA agent could easily pay the salary of a university professor, who officially got a monthly salary equivalent to twenty US dollars. This salary was not even regularly paid. That was why most professors were forced to sell their syllabi to students to survive, and they made students pay up front for their studies. This was beyond ridiculous.

Chapter 12

Until now, after her third year in Prague, Dorothy had an intimate relationship with Gilbert, the guy from the Congo Republic. They got married, had a baby boy named Michael, and lived together in the same student apartment. This time Dorothy's parents approved. They had no problem with that. They just did not want their daughter to be married to Thomas Kasusu, the son of their rivals, the Kasusus. That was all.

Dorothy's family liked Gilbert so much and proudly accepted his family from Brazzaville, who crossed the Congo River and came to arrange the traditional marriage of Gilbert and Dorothy. This was the way it was done here. Even when the concerned couple was not present, it was still possible for both families to arrange and celebrate the traditional marriage.

For this purpose, Gilbert first had to send a letter to Dorothy's father to tell him about his intention to marry his daughter. Gilbert also had to notify his parents about his move. If they agreed, then he could move forward. In the letter to Dorothy's parents, Gilbert must ask her father to send him a list of everything they needed him to bring on the day he or his family would come to marry their daughter.

Also, Dorothy had to prepare her parents about Gilbert. In this case, Dorothy's mother had already met Gilbert in person and liked him very much. She described him to her husband. So everything was already okay. Dorothy's father responded to Gilbert's request and sent a list containing the following things needed (on the father's side) to marry Dorothy: one new complete suit, a nice tie, a pair of size forty-two black shoes, a black hat, a big male goat, one machete, one five-liter bottle of good red wine, one bottle of whiskey, ten boxes of soda, twenty boxes of good local beer, and a sum of a thousand American dollars in cash.

On the mother's side they asked for: one high-quality loincloth, one beautiful head scarf, one nice pair of size thirty-seven shoes, one hoe, a rooster, one bunch of plantains, a fifty-kilogram sack of high-quality rice, a twenty-five-kilogram carton of high-quality dried salted fish, a carton of frozen chicken, a five-kilogram sack of salt, one gallon of vegetable oil, seven boxes of beer, four boxes of soda, a gallon of palm wine, and five hundred American dollars.

Before the day that Gilbert's family was expected to come for the traditional marriage, Dorothy's mother became very loud in her living area. She did everything in her power to let everybody know that her daughter Dorothy had found a real man in Europe, and her fiancé's family was coming to marry her in Kinshasa. This news was not only addressed to Thomas Kasusu and his family, but also to the people of her community who thought Dorothy would never get another man or get married. This was becoming a proud event in the life of the Tshiputu family.

The day of the traditional marriage between Gilbert and Dorothy arrived. All Dorothy's family members were already in the Tshiputus' house. Everybody was waiting for Gilbert's family from Brazzaville to arrive. At exactly five o'clock, as planned, the bus carrying Gilbert's family members arrived at the address indicated on the invitation. At this time, the joy was clear on the faces of Dorothy's mother and many family members. Everybody entered the house and was welcomed by the Tshiputu family.

After the traditional marriage was arranged, everybody accepted everything that Dorothy's family requested. At this time, Gilbert and Dorothy were officially and traditionally married. Gilbert was represented by his brother Henry, and Dorothy was represented by her cousin Anita, the daughter of her mother's sister.

The party was a success. There was enough food, drink, and music for all the guests of this traditional marriage of Gilbert and Dorothy. The party ended the next morning.

After six and half years in Prague, Gilbert had finished with distinction his studies of business management and accounting at University of Prague. He now had a master's degree in business management and accounting from the University of Prague in Czech Republic.

And right after his graduation, with the help of his consulate in Berlin, the reunited capital city of the Germans, Gilbert quickly received his repatriation ticket from the Congo Direction of Orientation and Scholarship to return to Brazzaville. He received a repatriation ticket with 150 kilograms for extra luggage. That was the kind of ticket the Congo Republic always sent to repatriate students who had finished their studies in foreign countries.

Gilbert was happy to return to Congo, but at the same time he was in pain to leave his wife and small boy. But Gilbert didn't have a choice. He had to go quickly back to Brazzaville to find a job so he would be able to prepare a place for Dorothy and their son to eventually come home to Congo.

After packing his things, Gilbert was ready to leave all his friends in the Congo community, his Czech friends, his wife Dorothy, and their son in Prague. The emotions were intense at Prague International Airport.

Gilbert was well-known in his community. He was a big activist for the Congo community in Prague. Nothing could be done without his knowledge or his participation. He knew everything and was loved by everyone in the Congo community of Prague. So everybody was there to say good-bye to the man who served his community and who was now going back to Congo, the country he would serve proudly by bringing Czech expertise and knowledge acquired here in Prague.

After all the formalities at the airport, Gilbert was ready to embark. He hugged his wife and kissed her and his twelve-month-old son. Dorothy had red eyes from crying. Gilbert hugged his Congo "brothers" and friends who accompanied him to the airport. Then he disappeared into the embarkation room.

Dorothy was left alone with her baby boy, Michael. She had to finish her studies before she could join her husband in Brazzaville. She still had three years left for that.

She and Gilbert had planned that, at the end of the next academic year, during the vacation period, Dorothy and her son, Michael, would be able to travel to Brazzaville. From there they would cross the Congo River to visit Dorothy's family and her daughter, Nisha, in Kinshasa. Hopefully by that time, Gilbert would be working.

Chapter 13

Gilbert was back in Brazzaville. This was an event for the Mavinga family. Gilbert's brother Henry and his parents decided to organize a party, celebrating Gilbert's return to Congo and his graduation.

They rented a facility in the city where the party would take place. Many people were invited to this party, mostly family members living in Brazzaville and other family friends. Before the party started, Henry, the oldest son of the Mavinga family, read the text honoring Gilbert's success and honoring the Mavinga family. "This is a moment of pride for our family. We all are meeting here because of this man, my young brother Mr. Gilbert Mavinga. He just came from Prague in Czech Republic, where he finished his studies. He graduated with honors from the department of economics at University of Prague and earned a master's degree in economic science with specialization in business management and accounting."

After the speech, everyone was pleased to start the party. Food and drinks were served, and the floor was set up for dancing. They celebrated all night and went back home early in the morning. Before leaving the party, most people said words of congratulations to Gilbert and his parents.

The party was over. It was now time for serious things. Gilbert had to find a job. But first he had to produce a complete dossier to the employment department of the Congo labor ministry. Once the dossier had been introduced in this ministry, it would then follow all the steps of the way to the final decision.

Everybody in Congo knew the famous *Porte 8* (or "Door 8") of the employment department of the Congo Labor Ministry. When you produced paperwork here, you had to wait two to five years before being appointed to a ministry department to start a job—unless you had someone who was powerful and could follow up on your dossier and quickly find a job for you.

With the help of his politician brother, who had a lot of connections—even when his party was no longer in power—Gilbert was able to get a job. Henry had quickly found a job for him, and now he worked as a high-ranking accountant for the national electricity company *Société Nationale d'Electricité* (SNE). This was a very well-paid job for Gilbert. He was hired as a cadre for this electricity company. With his position, he had a right to a company house and car.

With all the knowledge acquired in Czech Republic, he was able to show his class and get everybody's respect for the job well-done. The ground was paved for his family in Prague to join him. And when the vacation time came, Gilbert was able to send two travel tickets for his wife and son to come and spend time with him in Brazzaville.

Dorothy and little Michael got to Brazzaville and were so happy to see Gilbert in a good situation. They enjoyed meeting all Gilbert's family members they hadn't met before. Everybody liked Dorothy and said she was a very nice wife for Gilbert.

Then Gilbert, Dorothy, and Michael took a long weekend and crossed the Congo River to visit Dorothy's family and her daughter, Nisha, in Kinshasa. Because of work, Gilbert would not stay longer in Kinshasa; he would leave them and return to Brazzaville. Dorothy and little Michael would stay in Kinshasa for one month and then go back to Brazzaville for the last month of their vacation before returning to Prague.

In Kinshasa, the joy was clear when Dorothy's family saw their daughter after so many years of absence. They were very happy to meet Gilbert and little Michael. Dorothy was overjoyed to see Nisha, who was four now and beautiful. Nisha did not know who Dorothy was until they told her. "Nisha, this is your mother, Dorothy, and the young boy is your little brother, Michael. He is two years old now."

Nisha was so happy with all the presents Dorothy and Gilbert brought for her. In brief, it was a joy they hadn't seen before.

After Gilbert returned to Brazzaville, Thomas Kasusu and his family decided to come and say hello to Dorothy. They were connected because of little Nisha. And when Dorothy saw Thomas, she found him changed. Even when he was trying to impress her with money, he looked a little skinny for a rich man like him. Here, everybody who was rich was a little fat, especially in the belly.

Something is not right with Thomas's health, thought Dorothy.

The time spent in Kinshasa was very nice. But Dorothy's parents had decided to keep Dorothy's little boy, Michael, in Kinshasa. They argued that this way Dorothy would feel free and calm to finish her studies, like Gilbert did.

Gilbert was not against this idea; he was even the one to suggest that Dorothy leave Michael in Kinshasa with her mom. He said he would be able to come sometime to Kinshasa to visit them.

The plan was set. Dorothy would go back to Brazzaville alone, spend the rest of her vacation with her husband, and then return to Prague.

Chapter 14

When Dorothy returned to Prague after a very good vacation, she still thought about the time well spent with her husband in Brazzaville and also about the time she stayed in Kinshasa with her parents and her two kids.

Now her two kids would grow up in their grandparents' house, where Dorothy herself grew up. They would enjoy the same privileges that Dorothy had when she was growing up there.

For Dorothy, life was no longer the same. She felt more mature because she was married and was the mother of two growing kids. Even when she was attending university in Prague and studying hard, her heart was strongly positioned in Congo, where her family lived.

In Brazzaville, things went well for Gilbert until the end of the year. But then the change suddenly came to Brazzaville. The political situation in the country started to get worse. The present man in power, who promised to transform the Congo Republic into a little African

Switzerland, did not really do great things. The people's situation did not improve, and no little African Switzerland was built. People started requesting new elections to choose a new president and Parliament, because the five years that were given to this president and his government had expired. Constitutionally it was time for new elections.

But clearly the old man in power did not want to go to elections. He was even trying to extend his mandate by explaining that he still would build the little African Switzerland he had promised to the Congo people. But people were saying to him, "No way, we want elections now."

Because he could not see another way to stay in power, and because he was not so sure he would win again against his opponent, the powerful man and former president, he decided to take another strategy. The president in power sent his people to attack the former president's residence, saying that he was the one who was inciting people to revolt. But Mr. President didn't know that the former president was well prepared for this eventuality and was experienced to handle any kind of attack from his rival.

This was the beginning of the second civil war in Brazzaville that finally spread around the country. The first civil war had started during the time of the first democratic elections that brought this president into power. During this first one, conflict in Brazzaville was intense. It was practically impossible for people to go from one area to another. Brazzaville was divided into three rival zones: the Zulus, the Ninjas, and the Cobras. And in these zones everyone was suspicious of anyone who dared to cross their territory. Many people died just because they were trying to go to another territory to do business.

The conflict ended only after an international mediation. This conflict left the city with massive destruction, especially in the downtown areas of Brazzaville.

Even now people had short-term memory; they did not remember the atrocities that occurred during the first civil war. They were determined to start another big war.

Quickly the conflict escalated to a huge confrontation between troupes of the regular army, mostly the ex-militia Ninjas and the secretly well-trained ex-militia Cobras of the former president. The actual president was sure to do something quick, just to neutralize the former president's militia and arrest him. But he miscalculated the force that the former president had. He had been president of the Congo Republic for so long and had built strong personal relationships with presidents of many countries surrounding the Congo Republic, especially Angola and Gabon.

The conflict took another turn; it became a conflict between north and south. And this was bad for Gilbert, because when the conflict broke he was on a mission to the northern part of the country, which belonged to the former president's influential zone. He was on a mission to bring money for the salaries of agents who worked in this part of the country for SNE. Gilbert, other agents, and regular people who were originally from the south were all trapped in the middle of the conflict.

As one of the main accountants for SNE, he frequently had this kind of mission to different regions of the country. This mission was permanent, because Congo did not have special well-organized companies for the transfer of funds. That was why, every three months, accountants like Gilbert went on a special mission to bring money for salaries of SNE agents to different regions of the country. On each mission, the delegation traveled in solid jeeps and was escorted by a cohort of well-equipped army people.

The conflict between the army people and the former president's people, also well equipped, became very intense. The former president's people felt more comfortable because they were fighting in their fief. They talked in their regional tongue and were able to mobilize all the village people on their side. They incited village people to chase the enemy from the south everywhere in their region.

With this kind of hate message, Gilbert and other people from the south had to run away from this region very quickly. There was no other way to join Brazzaville except by running in the dense Congo forest, which was very dangerous. People could get bitten by a venomous snake, get devoured by a wild animal such as a lion, get swallowed alive by a python, get poisoned by a scorpion, or even get bitten by mosquitoes and die from malaria fever. These were only some of the possible dangers that Gilbert and other people were about to face. Also, they could get trapped by the ex-president's people, who chose to hide in the forest and attack by surprise the government's army people.

This was really going to look like survival of the fittest in the jungle. And it was not guaranteed that the conflict would end soon!

In the jungle, Gilbert and a few other people were on their own. They were running from the north side of the country to the south. From the place where they started their long and dangerous journey, they had to walk about 350 kilometers to reach Brazzaville. Because the conflict was so intense, they had to walk fast nonstop day and night. The daytime was better than the night, because they could watch their step. If they stepped on a viper tail, they could say bye to the rest of the group. That happened to one of the group members who died soon after he got bitten by a very poisonous viper. The body was left right where he fell down, and the group continued their walk south.

There was almost no time to think of eating. If they found any savage root or tuber, they had to take it and eat while running. During their run, no one was really allowed to use fire, because it would show their position to fighters. If they could not follow the group, then they stayed alone behind, and this was dangerous.

After three weeks in the jungle, the combat was still very intense and most people in the group were already feeling bad from insect bites, intensive walking, malnutrition, and other consequences related to this situation.

At about a hundred kilometers to Brazzaville, the unthinkable happened. Gilbert collapsed. He had been bitten many times over by mosquitos. Now he was trembling and sweating from a very high malaria fever. Nobody in the group knew how to help him since they had no medicines except some herbs and roots found in the jungle, which they could only use for minor cases of malaria.

In this jungle nobody could help him; everybody was fighting for their own survival. They had to run faster even when they were exhausted already. The sound of heavy artillery combat was easy to hear even deep in the jungle. The situation was so scary. Even the birds were no longer singing. Some recognizable animals were running in all directions and showing some signs of panic. In the cities and villages, people were absent on the streets and were barricaded for many weeks inside their houses. But even here, some people were dying from random bullets or bomb explosions on their houses.

Gilbert could not stand and walk. Nobody could wait for him except two members of the group who agreed to assist him. They found some dirty water to try to cool his body down. But Gilbert did not give any sign of improvement. He could not hear or speak. He was just dying. At about noon, Gilbert died. The two friends covered him with his own clothes and left him after saying a short prayer to God.

Meanwhile, in Brazzaville, combat was still intense. Gilbert's brother Henry Mavinga, who had been working for the party of the former president, was trying to get some news from his young brother who had gone to the north on a mission. But he could not get anything, because in Brazzaville it was impossible to move from one place to another. Those who tried paid for it with their own lives.

Many people had crossed the Congo River, abandoning everything they had to go to Kinshasa in the Democratic Republic of Congo, where the UNHCR had set up a refugee camp for them.

In Brazzaville, the exchange of rockets had destroyed almost all the buildings in town, mostly in the downtown area. Many buildings had just been rebuilt after they were destroyed during the first civil war. So they got destroyed for a second time.

It was the same situation in Pointe-Noire. The government's army people were trying to catch all people belonging to the ex-president's tribe. This was becoming an ethnic conflict. But in Pointe-Noire, Gilbert's parents did not have much of a hard time because they were in their province and in the government fief. But they could not walk freely on the streets because of sporadic exchanges between government groups and the ex-president's militia. Some people were getting hit by uncontrolled bullets. That was why the government had imposed a curfew, to help track all the ex-president's militia people.

Gilbert's parents tried to reach Henry by phone in Brazzaville to get some news about Gilbert, if any. But the connection between Pointe-Noire and Brazzaville became impossible because of the war. The family was simply separated from their two sons.

Finally, after many months of conflict and after destroying almost everything, the conflict came to an end, with a clear victory for the former president's camp. The former president got huge help from some African friends in power in countries surrounding the Congo Republic and also from one specific western country.

The old president who started everything ran away with all the members of his government and their families, leaving the country in the hands of one strong man who got back the power and governed without sharing it.

The two men who saw Gilbert dying in the jungle had finally arrived in Brazzaville. They brought the devastating news to the SNE office. Then the SNE office transferred the news to Gilbert's brother Henry. A radio communication was also read for his parents in Pointe-Noire. The news of Gilbert's death was heartbreaking for Gilbert's parents and family.

Chapter 15

In Prague, Dorothy was aware about the civil war that broke up in the Congo Republic, where her husband, Gilbert, lived and worked. During this war, she tried many times to get in touch with Gilbert, but it was really impossible to reach Brazzaville by phone because of the war. Nothing was working during this period.

But because she kept trying, she got lucky one day. She could talk for two minutes with Gilbert's brother Henry. Henry told her Gilbert was trapped in the northern part of the country, where he had gone on his company's mission. With this news, she wondered how Gilbert would reach Brazzaville. She knew that the conflict was becoming a north-south conflict and would certainly affect her husband, who was from the south but now trapped in the north.

She even tried one time to write a letter to Gilbert via his company, but she received no answer. She was in despair because she had tried everything she could, but there was no way she could get in contact with Gilbert.

After months, when the conflict was over and the communications came back to normal, she called

Brazzaville immediately to get news from her husband. They told her, "Gilbert was trapped in the conflict in the north, where he was on a mission. He ran in the big forest with other people, trying to reach Brazzaville by foot. But he did not make it. He died from high malaria fever in the jungle at about a hundred kilometers north of Brazzaville."

This was the most devastating news she had ever received. She screamed and cried like a baby. She fell on the ground and rolled over and over again. Her life changed dramatically and didn't have meaning anymore.

For weeks nobody could calm her down. All Congo students and their community in Prague were in a very sad mood. They collected money to help Dorothy travel to the Congo Republic via Kinshasa, where she planned to pick up her parents and then cross the Congo River to go to Brazzaville for the funeral in honor of her deceased husband.

At the time when she got the news of the devastating death of her husband, she was in her fourth year and had only one year before she got to the finish line of her studies. She was already doing her research work. By next year, she was sure to finish and defend her research in business management and accounting. Then she would get her master's degree like her husband did.

A week later, when she got to Kinshasa, she first organized a mourning night in her husband's memory. Many of her family members and friends attended. Everybody felt very sorry for her loss and was standing by her side.

After this event, she was ready to go with her parents to Brazzaville, but the situation in Brazzaville was not totally under control. In the town, there were still some pockets of resistance from the defeated old president's people. So the borders were still closed, and it was impossible to make the move to Brazzaville. She had to wait until the situation came back to normal and the borders reopened.

Meanwhile, when she was still mourning, she found out about Thomas Kasusu, her first child's daddy. She was told that after Thomas finished his finance studies at the University of Kinshasa, his father found him a very nice job in OFIDA. Thomas was making a lot of money, but he started dating different girls who were running after him just for the money. He had everything he needed: fast cars, beautiful villas, nice clothes, and a luxurious life.

Thomas could not resist the temptation of girls running after him. And after a routine testing of his blood requested by his job, Thomas was found to be HIV positive. A year later he developed AIDS. Since then he lost his job and had to sell all his valuables. Now he was back at his parents' house. He was always in his room and had lost a lot of weight. They tried to medicate him, but he quickly fell into a depression and the disease was developing very fast. His parents felt hopeless; they anticipated the worst.

This was more bad news for Dorothy. But even in her sad situation, she decided to go visit Thomas at his family's house. When she got there, they let her go in his room. There she found a skeleton of a man lying on the bed. At first Dorothy did not recognize Thomas. He sat up with a lot of difficulty. Then he said, "Hi, Dorothy. I heard you lost your husband in the Congo war. I am so sorry for you. Please accept my sincere condolences."

Dorothy answered, "Thank you for that. I am so sad, but when I heard about you, I decided to come and see you before I leave to go to Brazzaville."

Thomas added, "It's nice of you. How are Nisha and her little brother doing?"

Dorothy said, "I think they're okay. Michael knows his dad has passed away, and Nisha knows you're very sick. She told me you will be just fine."

Thomas said, "Thank you. She is such a beautiful girl. When are you going to Brazzaville?"

Dorothy responded, "As soon as the borders open again. After the mourning in Brazzaville, I will go back to Prague to continue my studies."

"When do you plan to finish them?"

"Next year if everything goes well."

"I wish you good luck!"

"Thanks."

They talked a bit longer, but with a lot of pain Dorothy finally had to leave him alone in his room. She was very moved when she returned home. With her own eyes she had seen how AIDS was consuming his former boyfriend and the father of her daughter, Nisha. She was very sad to think that both her children would live without their fathers.

When the borders finally opened, she crossed the Congo River with her parents to go to Brazzaville. When they arrived in Brazzaville, they saw a devastated city, with broken glass in almost all the buildings. In downtown Brazzaville, all high-rise buildings showed signs of bombings. In front of some of the buildings were posted clear warning signs, telling people to stay away because of the danger of buildings collapsing. Also they could still smell an odor of death in some broken buildings. This entire city looked like the aftermath of a powerful earthquake.

In Brazzaville they stayed at Henry's house, where all Gilbert's family and friends were gathering for one month in honor of Gilbert's memory. When people saw Dorothy and her parents, they started crying again. It was very sad to see how devastated Gilbert's parents were, but this was the destiny that was reserved for Gilbert. Nobody could change it.

Dorothy stayed one entire month in Brazzaville, mourning her husband. Her parents went back to Kinshasa after one week of mourning. Dorothy then used her courage to return to Prague. Henry rode with her to the airport. He said to her, "Keep up your courage, and go finish your studies. This is the way you can help your children, and Gilbert will always be proud of you."

Dorothy answered, "Thank you, Henry. I will."

Then she left for Prague.

Back in Prague, Dorothy was more focused on finishing her studies, even though she was still in deep mourning for her husband. In an effort to achieve her goal, she counted on the support of everybody around her. Her fellow department and all her professors provided support in this time of great need. Also, on a daily basis the Congo community in Prague and friends from everywhere came to Dorothy with their support.

All these actions gave Dorothy more faith in herself and the confidence to be strong and go ahead with her studies. That was why in the same year, she did her best to do much with her research and brilliantly pass to her final year in economics.

In this last year she would finish her studies, defend her research, and get her master's degree in business management and accounting. So Dorothy was very focused and busy. Every day she spent long hours in the department library, trying to fix all the issues related to her final work. This way she was able to put away, at least for now, all the grief related to the painful loss of her husband. She was so focused on her work that sometimes she had problems remembering what day of the week it was.

But before she finished writing the definitive conclusion of her work, she received the news of Thomas Kasusu's death. This came at the wrong moment. She was just forgetting the terrible loss of her husband and was finishing her research. That was when the new tragedy struck.

Even when she knew that Thomas would not live longer, she was still hoping that he would get better and maybe miraculously recover, regain his vitality, come back to full life, and take care of his daughter, Nisha.

This was more terrible news that destabilized Dorothy again for two full weeks. And one more time, with the encouragement of friends and the Congo community in Prague, she overcame this distress.

Dorothy was a widow with two kids without fathers. This was the main problem that now ruined Dorothy's heart. But there was nothing she could really do with this situation. She had to think positively and move on. This was the advice that everybody gave her to make her strong again and move on with her life.

After her two-week mourning time for the death of Thomas Kasusu, she finally went back to her primary occupation. She decided to work intensively to recoup the time she lost during this second fatal situation and finish her research. She was a little late according to the academic calendar, but the department gave her more time to get her work done.

⋆⋙○◎⋘⋆

The big moment came when Dorothy had to defend her final work in the department of economics at the University of Prague. Many people were invited to her defense, including the friends and Congo community members who had supported her in the bad periods of her life.

The large room of the economics department was packed with people. When Dorothy took the stage, the dean introduced her by giving her biography and also reminding people about what a courageous person Dorothy Tshiputu was to finish her studies after losing two very important people in her life.

Then Dorothy brilliantly defended her research, giving the results of her research and the conclusion of the work. At the end, Dorothy was given a series of questions. She answered all the questions professionally, and the audience gave her a deserving applause.

After this, the members of the academic jury deliberated in her favor. With distinction she was proclaimed master in economic sciences with a major in business administration and accounting at University of Prague. The joy was clear on Dorothy's face. She received congratulations from everybody in the room.

Then she went to a telephone booth and called her parents to tell them how she did with her defense. Her mother and father went crazy on the other side of the world, in Kinshasa. Dorothy even talked with her two children. All of them congratulated her for the brilliant success.

She waited three months for her diploma to be released from the Czech Ministry of Education. She was notified by her department to come get her diploma. She was very happy to hold her degree in her hands.

"Now it's time to go back home and start a professional life in Kinshasa," she said.

When she received the airplane ticket from her parents the next month, she started to pack her things. She was a little sad to leave Prague, the city she loves and in which she was educated. She loved Prague so much that sometimes she thought she would never leave this city. But in reality things were different. Certainly she had a story here, but at the same time she got to go back to the country where she had her roots and where all her family lived.

At the end of February, when Prague was in the middle of the cool season, Dorothy decided to leave Prague and return home to Kinshasa. She took time to say good-bye to all her people, including the department staff members, friends, and all the members of the Congo community in Prague.

At Prague International Airport, Dorothy was accompanied by friends from the Congo Republic and some Czech friends. After she finished all the formalities at the airport, she gave everyone a hug and waved to them before she went inside the waiting room.

A few minutes later she was on the airplane that belonged to Czech Airlines. It was taking her to Brussels, and from Brussels she would take Sabena Airlines to Kinshasa.

Chapter 16

Dorothy was happy to be back in Kinshasa and get reunited with her family and, more importantly, with her two kids. Nisha was now five years old, and Michael was three.

Dorothy knew very well she was left a widow with two children, and for now she had no job prospects. She had to take care of her two children, and this was going to be tough because her father was forced to retire by the new dictatorial regime that kicked out the regime of the previous dictator, who brutally ruled the country for thirty-two years. They didn't want people who had worked for the dictator to work with them.

So, the Democratic Republic of Congo had been once freed from a brutal dictator, who was kicked out by an easy rebellion that started in the east of the country. This rebellion was helped by western countries, which did not like the old and sick dictator anymore. They armed small countries surrounding the DR Congo so they could help the rebellion move forward and overthrow the unwanted dictator.

But even when the rebellion was strongly equipped, the dictator's army did not even fight. This was because the army did not have good logistics, and most of the soldiers did not want to fight for a dictator who was not treating them well—except his own special division, composed mostly of people from his native village.

Inside the country, there was also a nonviolent opposition that had been fighting the dictator for long time, but because they did not have any military support they could not do much. This internal peaceful opposition just helped the rebellion to get easily to their goal. They told people and soldiers serving in the dictator's army to not resist the rebellion's army groups and let them enter the DR Congo to overthrow the dictator. The DR Congo people had enough of the dictator who had completely destroyed the country and killed many valuable people that tried to oppose him.

When this rebellion started in the eastern part of the country, it was very brutal. They destroyed many infrastructures and killed so many innocent people. The army recruited a lot of children and gave them much marijuana, so they could go anywhere and do anything they asked them to do. That was why young soldiers raped women, old and young. They killed any suspected male they found in the family and enrolled by force any young boy they found.

It was horrific, because in most rape cases the victims were left contaminated with HIV. Many ladies had their intimate organs mutilated by those who raped them. And the consequences were enormous; kids were left orphans on streets, living by themselves. What could a five-year-old girl, with infirmity in the leg, do alone on the street?

Most of these atrocities were done in the eastern part of the country, but also in the north and a little bit in the center. Kinshasa and a few other provinces did not have many rapes and mutilations, but they had a lot of arbitrary killings and other bad things related to the new dictator's rules. People were terrorized by the fury of the new occupants. They were strongly armed and for any reason kid soldiers would kill anybody who was suspected by them.

Since the big revolts and the civil war that emerged during the time of the country's independence in the 1960s, this was the first really violent movement that the DR Congo had to boost out of power a dictator. Also, it was important to know that this rebel movement to kick out the dictator in the DR Congo started almost in the same period as the first civil war that broke out in the Congo Republic during their first democratic elections, which brought to power the old man who just got kicked out by the recent conflict in which Gilbert had lost his life.

Now in Kinshasa, Dorothy was living in the rhythm of the new dictatorial regime. She could not find a job, especially when her father was no longer in the business. There were no jobs in all the country. New graduate students and old graduates were in the same situation. The new regime blamed the previous regime for the devastating situation they found when they took power. They said they had found only forty-seven US dollars in the Central Bank and nothing else except the colossal debt with which the country was left. And the corruption was deeply institutionalized. The new regime didn't know how to stop the corruption. The situation was very bad for everybody, including Dorothy and her family.

To avoid getting into a worse living situation, Dorothy's parents decided to sell all they had and then move to the village located in the eastern part of the country. They planned to sell their house, cars, and all their furniture. And with the money they expected to collect, they would move to their village in the southeastern part of the DR Congo. Back in their village, they planned to build a huge farm that would make them one of the very serious producers of cow meat, pork meat, goat meat, sheep meat, chicken meat, eggs, corn and cassava flours, fruits, and vegetables.

This was a very enticing project for Dorothy. They were so certain that after the previous dictator was kicked out of the country, the new regime would slowly but surely fix the bad economic situation left by the previous regime. And with this farm project in their village, they would become one of the best producers of farm products in the area and would probably live a better life.

They knew that the security in the country, especially in the east, had returned to normal. People were doing activities they used to do without getting attacked by any army groups. According to the new DR Congo government at that time, the security was very good and had improved to avoid any kind of attack from armed groups, if any.

With this kind of confidence given to the Tshiputu family by the new regime, and because they believed in what the new regime said about the capacity they had to keep the entire territory of the country secured, the Tshiputu family became so determined to do what they decided. And that was done.

◦≡◦⊂≡◦

After a few months, when they had sold everything and money was in their hands, the Tshiputu family moved to their village in the southeastern part of the DR Congo. Back in their village, Dorothy and her kids were very impressed by what they saw. Dorothy's young brothers were also happy to live in their village.

Here people had large living spaces, there was much land, and people knew each other and spoke the same tongue. When Dorothy's father was still in the government business, he was clever enough to build a house in his native village. Now this house was there to help them start organizing their farm project.

In just six months, the Tshiputu family had a big farm where Dorothy's father had recruited some village people to work for him. There were people to work in the livestock farm with cows, pigs, goats, sheep, and chicken, and there were people to work in the plantations of cassava, corn, tomatoes, eggplant, beans, peanuts, and more. Everything was going well, but they did not know that pretty soon a new war would be coming to that part of the country.

After just two years of solid farming activity, a new rebellion to the new regime was formed. This one started also in the east of the DR Congo. Their goal was to overthrow this new dictator because they said he did not keep the contracts signed before he took power in Kinshasa. But the new man in power in Kinshasa was sure of himself. He was trying to show people that he had control of the situation, which was just not true.

Rapidly the rebels attacked by surprise all the eastern provinces of the DR Congo. The Tshiputus' village was among the first villages to be attacked by the rebels. This rebellion was more violent than the first that brought in this new dictator.

They used the same techniques that were used with the previous rebellion. When they got to a village, they raped women, old and young, in front of their husbands, fathers, and children, and they killed all adult men and enrolled by force young boys into the army. Also, they stole everything they saw in the house. They destroyed farms and maintained chaos and desolation in the village.

This was exactly what happened to Dorothy and her family. They were trapped in this tragedy. When the rebels got into their house, they raped Dorothy's mother right in front of her husband. Because Dorothy's father did not want to watch them raping his wife, like they told him to do, they killed him with one bullet in the head. Dorothy tried to escape, but they took her and her eight-year-old girl and raped them too. And because her mother was fighting so much, the commander decided to shoot her also in the head. All the young boys in the house were screaming and crying. The scene was unbearable: dead bodies all around and blood everywhere.

When the rebels were done, they took all three of Dorothy's brothers and left with them to an unknown destination. Dorothy was in pain because she had been raped by almost eleven people. And her little girl was raped by the commander himself. Dorothy begged them to leave her brothers, but they refused and ran away in their pickup truck.

The scene was macabre to watch. Dorothy and Nisha, both violently raped, and her terrified little boy, Michael, were left with two dead parents and three brothers taken to an unknown destination.

On the second day of this devastating incident, the Red Cross arrived. They took the bodies of Dorothy's parents, along with Dorothy, Nisha, and Michael, to the nearest hospital camp for first aid. Dorothy and her daughter had been badly raped, so they were transferred to a big-town hospital for more care.

After months, Dorothy was still without news of her three brothers. She was now living in a refugee camp with her traumatized daughter and son. There were many other women from different villages who had also been raped by the same army groups and were transferred to the same camp as Dorothy. They stayed about three years in this refugee camp, and still Dorothy did not know where her three brothers might be. She probably would never see them again.

In the meantime, with the new techniques of early detection of the HIV virus, Dorothy had been found positive with the virus. Her daughter, Nisha, was lucky; she was not diagnosed with the HIV virus. With this news, Dorothy was completely devastated, and her life was destroyed.

Every night she had insomnia, because she kept seeing the scene where she and her daughter got raped, her parents were killed, and her three brothers were taken by rebels. She lost any desire to live. She didn't know what to do with herself. She thought she was going to kill herself. Every day she was very sad and crying.

But after many months of intense therapy, with the help of international organizations, she was able to accept life with this virus. The international group for assistance to the victims of war in the DR Congo assisted her in her fight against the HIV virus, and it helped her live some semblance of a normal life.